John Adams

Am I in your light?

Kitty's aria from Act I scene 2
of the opera *Doctor Atomic*

Libretto by Peter Sellars
drawn from original sources

Piano Vocal Score

for Soprano
Revised Piano Reduction

HENDON MUSIC

BOOSEY & HAWKES

DISTRIBUTED BY

HAL•LEONARD®

7777 W. BLUEMOUND RD. P.O. BOX 13819 MILWAUKEE, WI 53213

www.boosey.com
www.halleonard.com

Am I in your light?
DOCTOR ATOMIC
Kitty's aria from Act I, Scene 2

Libretto by
PETER SELLARS

Music by
JOHN ADAMS
revised piano reduction

(Kitty and Oppie are alone in their living room. He is reading documents, oblivious to her.)

Tranquillo (♩ = 58)

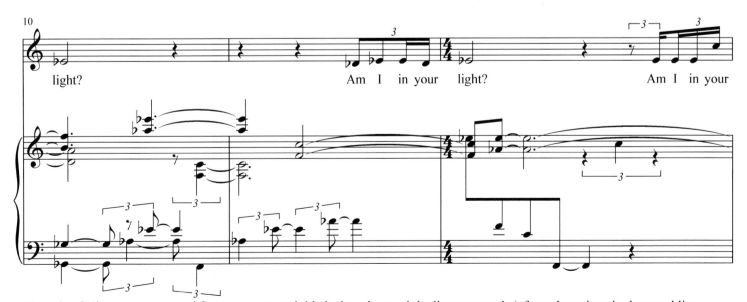

The role of Kitty was composed for a soprano, and this is the aria as originally composed. A few adaptations in the vocal line were made for a mezzo-soprano when cast in the role.

birds, ___ and ___ eve - ning warns ___ us, ___ warns us beau - ti - f'lly of

death. ___ Slow - ly ___ I bend o - ver you, ___

slow - ly, slow - ly your breath ___ runs rhy - thms through my blood

as if I said I love you, and you should

See how love al - ters the liv - ing face

go spin the im - mor - tal coin through time

watch the thing flip through space tick tick

tick tick tick tick tick tick.

(childlike)

(l.v. till m. 95)

(gently)

dim.